Let's Practic

ABCs

Contents

Brighter Child®
An imprint of Carson Dellosa Education
PO Box 35665
Greensboro, NC 27425 USA

ISBN 978-1-4838-4601-9

08-139201151

The Letter Aa

Trace and write.

Color the apples with **A** or **a**.

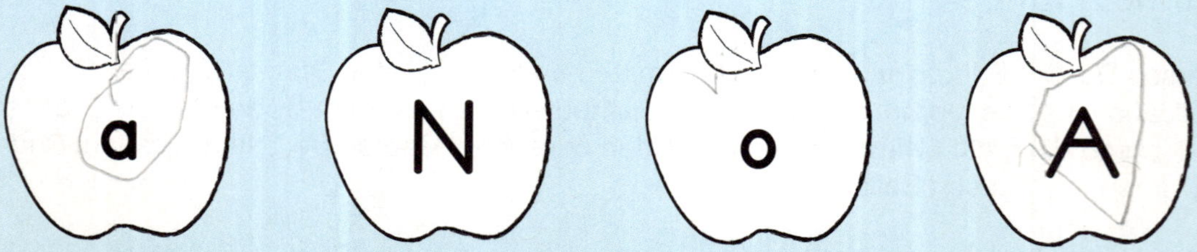

The Letter Bb

Trace and write.

Bb

bear

bed

Color the pictures whose names begin with the sound you hear at the beginning of **bear**.

The Letter Cc

Trace and write.

C C

c c

Trace the lines from left to right.

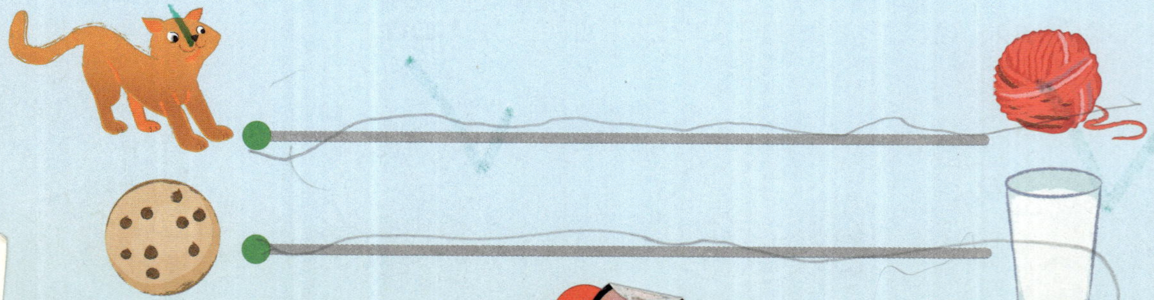

The Letter Dd

Trace and write.

Dd

D D

d d

Follow **D** and **d** to get the dolphin to the treasure!

The Letter Ee

Trace and write.

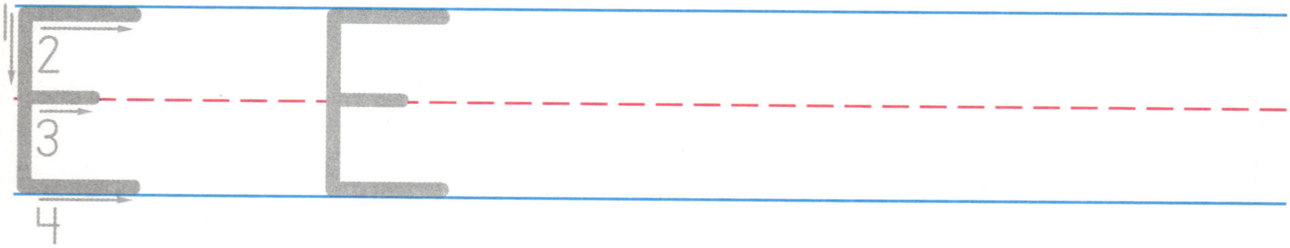

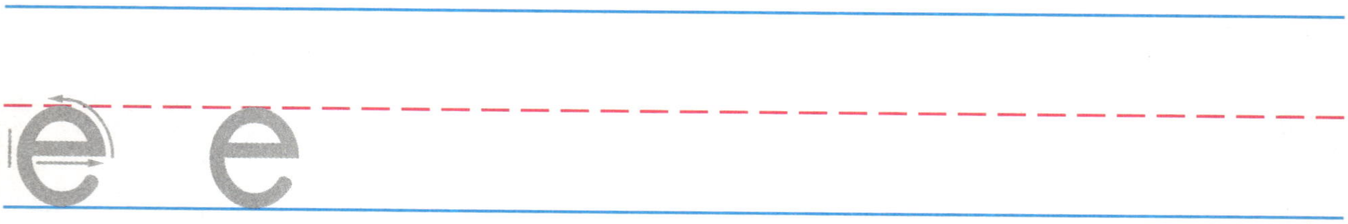

Circle the eggs with **Ee**.

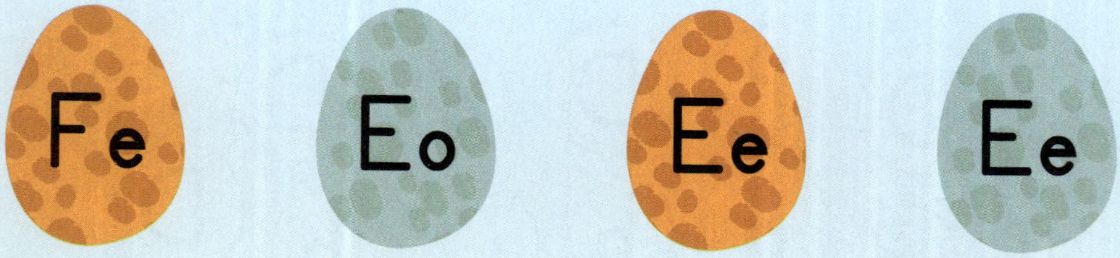

The Letter Ff

Trace and write.

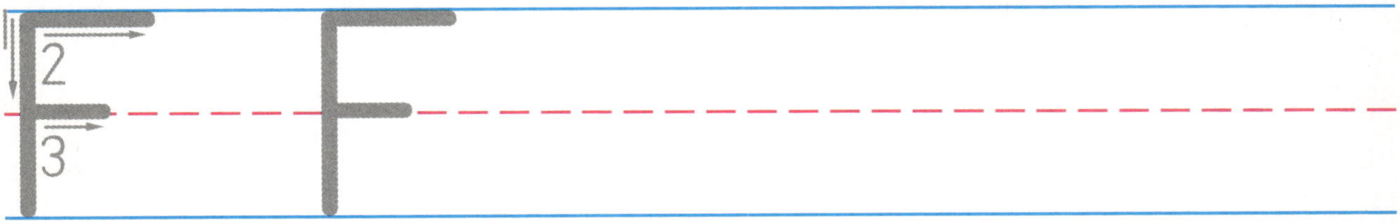

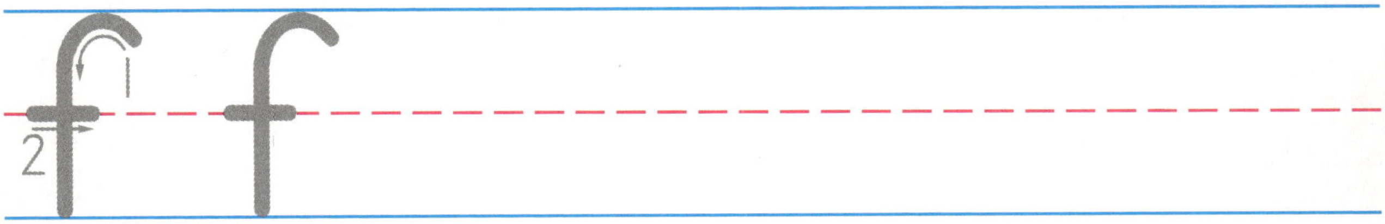

Find and circle each **F** and **f**.

The Letter Gg

Trace and write.

Circle the gift that is different.

The Letter Hh

Trace and write.

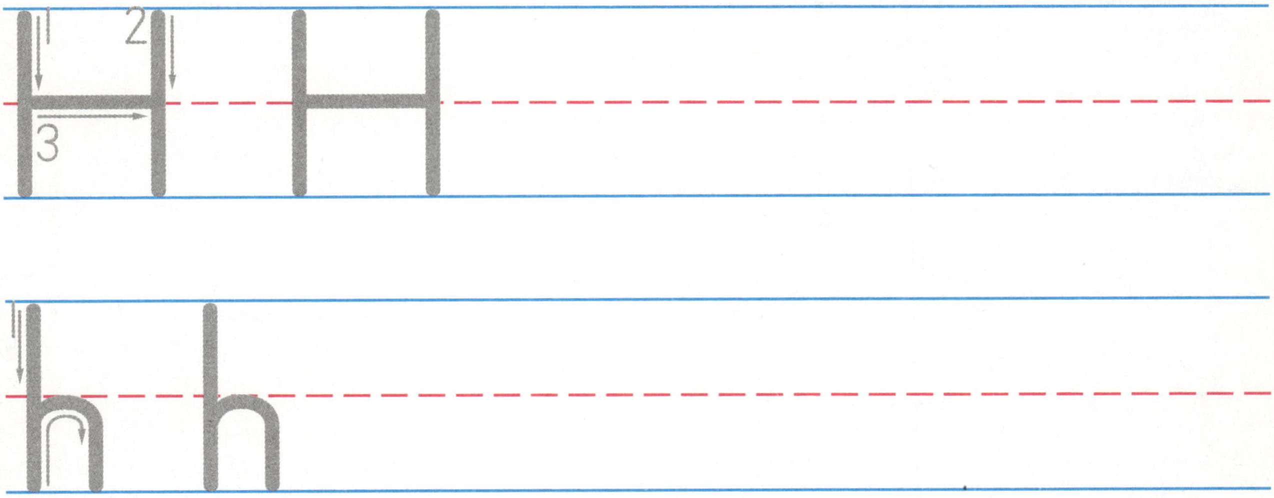

Follow **H** and **h** to get the horse to the carrots.

The Letter Ii

Trace and write.

What is the opposite of winter? Draw a picture.

The Letter Jj

Trace and write.

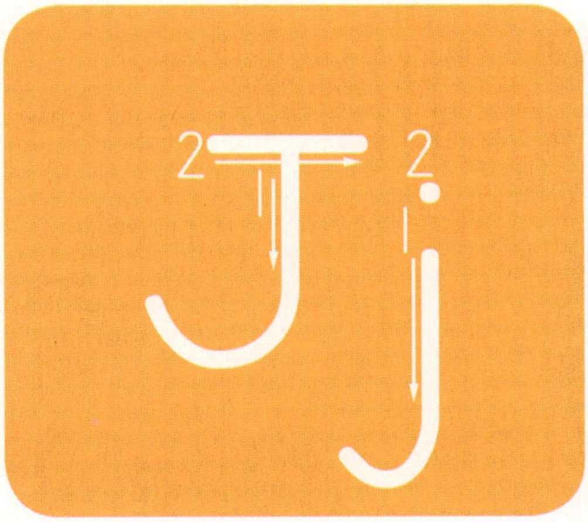

Circle the jewels with **J** or **j**.

The Letter Kk

Trace and write.

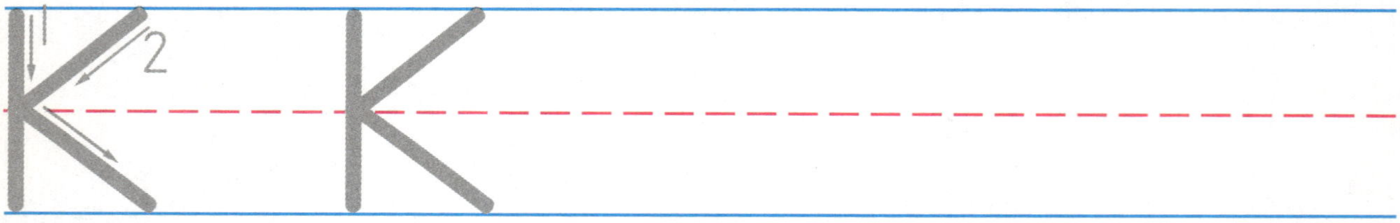

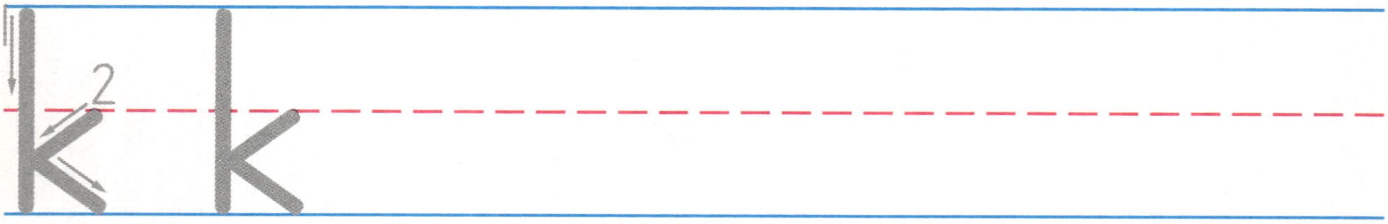

Color the picture whose name rhymes with **king**.

The Letter Ll

Trace and write.

L l

L L

l l

Circle the lowercase letter that matches **L**.

The Letter Mm

Trace and write.

Mm

M M

m m

Find and circle each **M** and **m**.

The Letter Nn

Trace and write.

N N

n n

Trace the lines from left to right.

The Letter Oo

Trace and write.

Color the picture with a matching letter above.

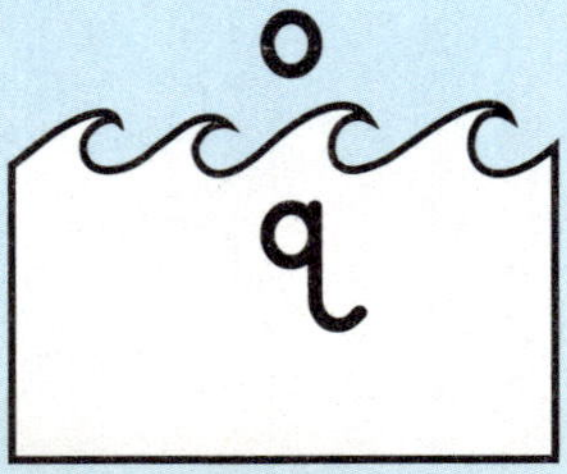

The Letter Pp

Trace and write.

popcorn

penguin

P P

p p

Circle pictures whose names begin with the sound you hear at the beginning of **penguin**.

The Letter Qq

Trace and write.

Circle the animal that **quacks**.

The Letter Rr

Trace and write.

Find and circle each **R** and **r**.

The Letter Ss

Trace and write.

S S

s s

Circle the words that rhyme with **snake**.

cake

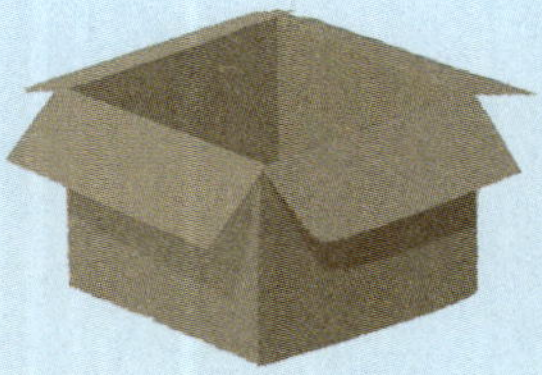

box

hose

rake

The Letter Tt

Trace and write.

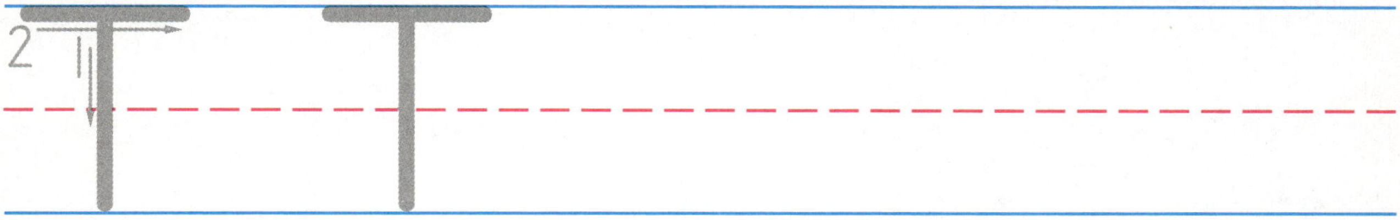

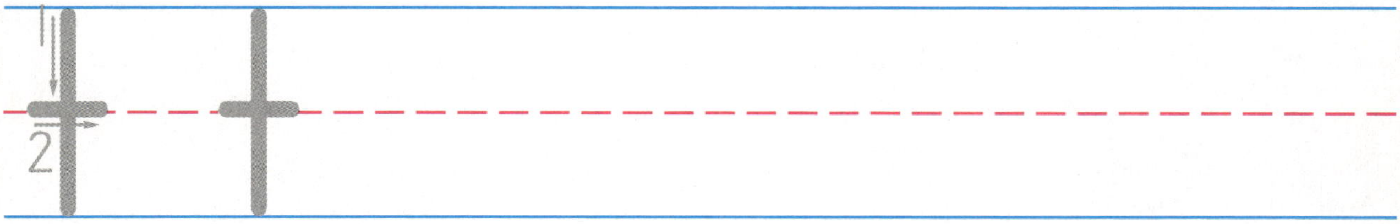

Trace the lines from left to right.

The Letter Uu

Trace and write.

Circle the word that tells where the arrow is pointing.
Find **u** in each circled word.

up

down

over

under

The Letter Vv

Trace and write.

Circle pictures whose names begin with the sound you hear at the beginning of **vase**.

The Letter Ww

Trace and write.

Find **w** in each word. Act out each action.
Can a partner guess it?

wink wave waddle wash

The Letter Xx

Trace and write.

Circle pictures whose names end with the sound you hear at the end of **six**.

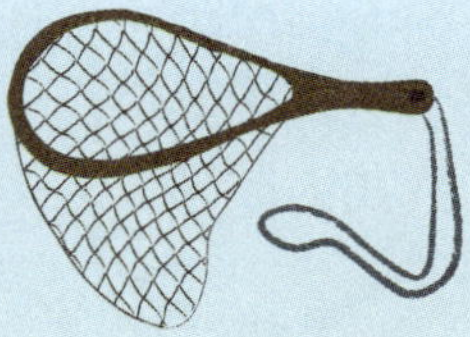

The Letter Yy

Trace and write.

Y Y

y y

Color the picture with a matching letter pair.

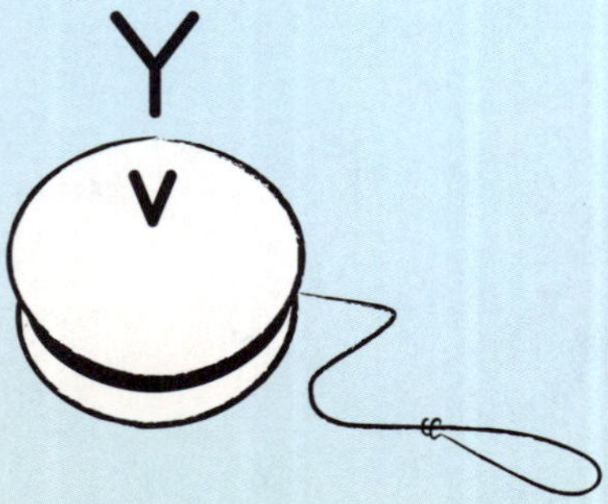

The Letter Zz

Trace and write.

Circle the zoo animals. Draw a box around the farm animals.

ABC Order

Connect the dots from **A** to **Z.** Color the picture.

ABC Order

Connect the dots from **a** to **z**. Color the picture.

Uppercase & Lowercase Letter Pairs

Match the uppercase and lowercase letters.

	B	a
	D	b
	A	d
	F	l
	E	e
	L	f

Uppercase & Lowercase Letter Pairs

Write the missing letter in each pair.

r	N	V
q	t	
S	U	w
z	P	o
X		Y

I Know the Alphabet

Find and circle the letters from **A** to **Z**.